IMAGES
of America

TROLLEYS
UNDER THE HUB

A feature of the trolley subway was the Information Booth, the only one on the entire system, which was located at the Park Street Station on the southbound platform. (Courtesy of David Rooney.)

IMAGES
of America

TROLLEYS
UNDER THE HUB

Frank Cheney and Anthony M. Sammarco

ARCADIA

First published 1997
Copyright © Frank Cheney and Anthony M. Sammarco, 1997

ISBN 0-7524-0907-7

Published by Arcadia Publishing,
an imprint of the Chalford Publishing Corporation,
One Washington Center, Dover, New Hampshire 03820.
Printed in Great Britain

Library of Congress Cataloging-in-Publication Data applied for

Looking east from Perkins Square in South Boston, this view shows the section of the street rising from Dorchester Street which was often referred to as Pill Hill, because of the large number of doctors' offices along that section of East Broadway.

Contents

In this photograph, passengers awaiting their trolley are sitting on wooden benches at the southbound entrance to the Park Street Subway Station in the summer of 1901. The outbound-side track was later to be converted for use by the elevated trains from 1901 to 1908. (Courtesy of David Rooney.)

Introduction

It is with a sense of history repeating itself that we observe the one hundredth anniversary of the completion of Boston's first major construction project, the Tremont Street Subway, while the City is in the midst of another remarkably similar project known as the "Big Dig." Both projects consist of three major components: a major north-south tunnel through the downtown business district, an under-harbor tunnel to East Boston, and a large bridge across the Charles River near the North Station. Certainly there are lessons from the last century's project which could benefit the present-day project if applied with due consideration.

What were the factors which led the City of Boston, which considered itself the "Athens of America" and the "Hub of the Universe," according to local dignitaries, to undertake such a major project at the end of the last century? The answer is the acute and growing traffic congestion in the downtown area, especially in the heart of the business and shopping district along Tremont Street from Boylston Street through Scollay and Haymarket Squares to the North Station. Tremont Street at Park Street and Scollay Square had long been the downtown terminal point for the trolley car line from the areas north, south, and west of the Central Business District, and by the spring of 1895, one hundred and eighty-three streetcars per hour were passing the corner of Tremont and Park Streets in addition to the other traffic; a local journalist observed that the fastest way to get from Boylston Street to Scollay Square was to walk along the roofs of the trolley cars. Studies begun in 1891 concluded that only an elevated railway system, along with a subway through the main downtown shopping area where elevated trains were not desirable, could hope to alleviate the congestion. To remedy the situation, the state legislature passed Chapter 548 of the Acts of 1894 creating the Boston Transit Commission, a joint body of the Commonwealth and the City of Boston.

The commission was given the task of designing and building a north-south subway under Tremont Street from Shawmut Avenue through Scollay and Haymarket Squares to the North Station, with a short branch under Boylston Street to the Public Garden near Arlington Street; an under-harbor tunnel from Scollay or Adams Squares to Maverick Square in East Boston; and a drawbridge over the Charles River connecting Causeway Street in Boston's North End with City Square in Charlestown. The drawbridge would accommodate general traffic, streetcars, and elevated trains. The tunnels were to be operated with trolley cars, at least initially. Also included in Chapter 548 was the creation of the Boston Elevated Railway Company, which was empowered to build and operate elevated railways in the city of Boston. The transit commission undertook its task quickly. On the morning of March 28, 1895, two gentlemen strolled down the steps of the statehouse and across the Common to the Boylston Street side of the Public Garden, where a group of people stood around a wooden stake which had been driven into the turf. One of the gentlemen was Governor Frederick Greenhalge, and the other was his secretary. The two stood before the stake which marked the entrance ramp to the new subway. The governor said a few words to Howard A. Carson, chief engineer of the Transit Commission, and turned a spadeful of earth. He then handed the spade to Mr. Carson, who turned the second spadeful of earth. A few moments later the laborers of the Jones and Meehan Company of Boston began the actual construction work on the subway as the governor walked back to the statehouse. Edward Upton Curtis, the mayor of Boston, was too busy to attend the groundbreaking for America's first subway.

On December 7, 1896, the West End Street Railway Company, the operator of Boston's extensive streetcar system, signed a twenty-year lease with the transit commission for the use of the subway. The first section of the subway, from the Public Garden entrance as far as Park Street Station, opened on September 1, 1897. On December 12, 1897, the state railroad commission approved the lease of the West End Street Railway Company to the new Boston Elevated Railway Company, thus clearing the way for the use of the Tremont Street Subway by elevated trains. It should be mentioned that a major stockholder in both the West End and Boston Elevated Companies was Eben M. Jordan, Boston's leading merchant, who owned the Jordan Marsh Department Store and was an ardent promoter of Boston's planned elevated railway system.

The remainder of the Tremont Street Subway, from Park Street through Scollay, Adams, and Haymarket Squares to the North Station, opened on September 3, 1898, having taken only three years and six months to complete. The 2 and 1/4 miles of subway with five stations cost $4,160,024.52, well under the original estimate of five million dollars. This was the basis for the eventual Green Line system. The other two components of the transit commission-mandated project are beyond the scope of this story, and final mention of them will be made here. The second component was the Charlestown drawbridge, which opened to the public on November 27, 1899. The bridge, which is still in daily use, is 1,970 feet long and 100 feet wide, with a 240-foot-long swing-span, which weighs 1,200 tons. The bridge provided four lanes for general traffic, two streetcar tracks, and two elevated railway tracks and cost $1,453,284.04. The third component of the project, the East Boston tunnel, which extended from Scollay Square to Maverick Square in East Boston, was 7,500 feet in length with three stations, cost $3,037,142.53, and opened on December 30, 1904. Originally operated with trolley cars, it was converted to use regular subway trains in April 1924.

Returning to the Tremont Street subway, we find that trolley cars on twenty-seven routes from all parts of the metropolitan area ran into the subway in its early years. One could board cars at the Park Street or Scollay Square Stations for such diverse destinations as Brookline, Newton, Cambridge, South Boston, Arlington, Dorchester, Somerville, Jamaica Plain, Malden, Revere, and Lynn. The Transit Commission proudly announced that 210 trolley cars per hour were serving Park Street Station with no back-ups or congestion. On June 10, 1901, elevated trains on the Dudley Street to Sullivan Square route, the forerunner of today's Orange Line, began operation through the subway and was later joined by the trains of the Atlantic Avenue Loop Lines on August 22, 1901. Operation of elevated trains through the Tremont Street Subway would continue until they were rerouted into the new Washington Street tunnel on November 30, 1908, at which time the Tremont Street Subway returned to exclusive use by trolley cars.

Increasing ridership, combined with growing traffic congestion caused by growing use of the automobile, would lead to construction of several extensions to the original subway over the years. The Lechmere Viaduct Line, extending from the North Station to Lechmere Square in East Cambridge, opened on June 1, 1912. It was followed by the Boylston Street Subway, which extended from the Public Garden entrance of the old subway to Kenmore Square and opened on October 3, 1914. At this time there still were twenty routes using the subway. The extension of the Boylston Street Subway through Kenmore Square opened on October 23, 1932. The Huntington Avenue subway, which extended from Copley Square to Northeastern University, began operation on February 16, 1941, just in time to carry record war-time crowds.

In order to meet the challenge of ever increasing ridership, the Boston Elevated Company and the Transit Commission completed all the engineering plans for conversion of the central subway system to operation with rapid-transit trains in late 1929. The Blue Line had undergone a similar successful conversion in 1924. However, the 1929 financial Depression put these plans on hold until they were revived by the Metropolitan Transit Authority in 1962–1963. The final addition to what is now the Green Line system opened on July 4, 1959, when the Highland Branch, extending from Kenmore Square out to the Riverside Station and Route 128 in Newton, began operation with PCC trolley cars over the former commuter rail line of the Boston and Albany Railroad.

On September 1, 1947, the Boston Elevated Railway Company was replaced by the publicly-owned Metropolitan Transit Authority (MTA), which planned major improvements and additions to the Green Line system, including the enlargement of Park Street Station, the construction of two additional tracks to eliminate the bottleneck between Park Street and Scollay Square, and a new subway under Stuart Street from Copley Square to the tunnel entrance at Broadway and Tremont Streets. These planned projects received legislative approval but no funding. During 1963, as part of the massive Government Center development project, the subway through Scollay Square and Adams Square was rebuilt, eliminating several sharp curves. This was the last major improvement to the Green Line, aside from cosmetic improvements to the stations carried out in recent years.

In August of 1964 the Massachusetts Bay Transit Authority (MBTA) succeeded the MTA, and on August 26, 1965, the MBTA re-designated the Central Subway System as the Green Line System. Over the years many routes were removed from the Green Line subways, as the Red and Orange Rapid Transit Lines were extended into areas formerly served by trolley cars running directly downtown. As late as 1938 there were ten routes using the Green Line subways, with eight routes still feeding into the subway as recently as 1948. The year 1997 finds only four routes still serving Green Line riders.

While the MBTA at first enthusiastically announced major improvements to the Green Line based on plans drawn up by the former MTA, including the Stuart Street Subway and an extension from Lechmere Square into Somerville as well as a new light-rail line on Washington Street to feed into the Green Line, these plans have all been shelved, and in fact two heavily-used branches of the Green Line—the Watertown and Arborway Lines—have been abandoned in an attempt to divert riders away from the Green Line and reduce the number of riders using the system. Aside from purchasing new cars to replace worn out equipment and minimal upgrading of track and power facilities, Green Line management has made no major changes to the system, as the MBTA's primary goal in recent years has become the improvement and expansion of suburban commuter rail services. However, the Green Line system still carries far more riders than any other section of the MBTA's extensive rail system, and has played a major role in maintaining the viability of Boston's Downtown Center through the century.

One

Trolleys under the Hub:
the Beginning

This 1891 view of Tremont Street, looking south with the Park Street Church on the right and the old Horticultural Hall on the left, was taken from the Tremont House. Most of the streetcars in this photograph are horse-drawn ones, with only a few electric cars in sight. This section of Tremont Street had three tracks to handle the heavy streetcar traffic.

This view of Tremont Street in 1903, looking north from the corner of West Street, shows the noted Boston jewelry firm of Shreve, Crump and Low on the right, and the four-story Tremont House built by Isaiah Rogers in 1829 can be seen in the center of the photograph, just beyond the Park Street Church. Once considered Boston's leading hostelry, the Tremont House would be demolished in 1893 to make way for the Tremont Building, an eleven-story office building.

In this view looking north on Tremont Street from Boylston Street, the Cross Town Trolley is headed for Grove Hall in Roxbury, by way of Copley Square and Dudley Street. The handsome cast-iron fence of the Boston Common, seen in the foreground, was "temporarily" removed during construction of the subway, but never reinstalled.

In this view of Tremont Street, looking south from School Street, most of the streetcars are electrically powered and still dominate the traffic. Notice the large number of people waiting along the sidewalk in front of the Old Granery Burial Ground for their streetcar. There was usually a crowd waiting at this point, since so many trolley lines from the suburbs terminated here, in addition to the through-lines running from Dorchester and Roxbury to Charlestown and Malden, which passed through this section of Tremont Street.

This 1894 photograph, taken from the steps of the Park Street Church, shows the entrance to the Boston Common on the right. It is easy to see the conditions that led to the construction of the Tremont Street Subway. As far as the eye can see, trolley cars dominate the street, creating great congestion, since they were the primary means of reaching the business and retail district.

The usual parade of streetcars is under way in this 1895 view, which shows a Back Bay-Marlborough Street horsecar heading to Scollay Square. This, Boston's last horsecar route, was discontinued on December 24, 1900. Interestingly, the Brookline car in front of the horsecar displays a Tremont House destination sign on its roof, although that famous hotel had just been demolished.

The junction of Tremont and Pleasant Streets and Shawmut Avenue later became part of Broadway. This November 2, 1896 scene shows construction under way on the subway's Tremont Street entrance, which would undergo many changes over the years.

This 1896 view of Tremont Street looks north towards Boylston Street. While construction of the subway is carried on beneath the street, traffic continues to move along the surface, although construction equipment occupies the right-hand side of the street.

On April 21, 1896, at the corner of Tremont and Boylston Streets , excavations of the subway by the Boston construction firm of Jones and Meehan were well under way. While various construction firms worked on different sections of the subway, all the work was carried out under the close supervision of the Transit Commission's own engineers, who were led by Howard A. Carson.

On the morning of March 4, 1987, a severe explosion rocked the corner of Tremont and Boylston Streets, wrecking two streetcars and damaging several others. Seven people were killed and over forty injured. The two horses pulling the Back Bay horsecar in the foreground were also killed. The cause of the blast was determined to be gas seeping into the subway excavation from a leaking main, a situation for which the gas company was held liable. The partly-completed subway structure escaped damage since the force of the blast was directed upward, as can be seen in this photograph.

Five months after the explosion, the corner of Tremont and Boylston Streets had been repaired and the subway completed at this point. In just three weeks, the Brookline trolley turning onto Boylston Street would be running underground. The lady with the umbrella in this August 12, 1897 photograph is protecting her fair complexion from the sun, as it was unfashionable to be suntanned in the 1890s. Boston policemen would continue to wear the "bobby" helmets as seen here until 1919.

This photograph, taken at Tremont Street at King's Chapel on May 12, 1896, shows a Back Bay horsecar passing an electric trolley bound for Union Square, Somerville. The wooden bridgework above the sidewalks supported a conveyor system in which large buckets on a moving cable were used to remove excavated dirt from the subway and to deliver cement for the sidewalls and foundation. This method eliminated the use of numerous dump-wagons, which would have added to the already heavy traffic.

This view looking down on the intersection of Tremont, Beacon, and School Streets on June 11, 1896, shows the new eleven-story office building nearing completion on the site of the Tremont House Hotel. A section of the construction conveyor can be seen over the sidewalk on the right.

This view of Tremont Street looking north toward Boylston Street was taken on May 8, 1896. A noticeable feature of construction projects in this era was the total lack of effort to seal off construction work from the general public, which was a real plus for sidewalk superintendents!

In this May 13, 1897 photograph, we see an electric car hauling workmen, rails, and supplies into the Public Garden entrance of the subway on Boylston Street. The subway would not open to the public for another four months.

On the morning of September 1, 1897, America's first subway opened to the public when Car Number 1752 rolled down the entrance ramp at the Public Garden just before 6 am. The car had come in from Allston via Pearl Street, in Cambridge, and carried over one hundred riders, many of whom rode on the running boards. The motorman was James Reed (right), a former Sierra Nevada Indian fighter, and his conductor was George Truffant (left). The gentlemen posed here at the Allston Car House with their car several hours after the historic event.

On the first day of operation, the subway entrance at the Public Garden found trolleys from Cambridge, Brookline, and Meeting House Hill in Dorchester carrying crowds of eager riders who wished to see Boston's new subway. It would be seven years before New York City would open its first subway in 1904, finally catching up with the "Hub of the Universe," as Boston liked to style itself.

The "Bellmouth," or underground bridge south of Boylston Street Station, allowed cars destined for Tremont Street or Shawmut Avenue to reach their proper exit tracks without crossing in front of one another. Notice how brightly-lit the subway is, in addition to being whitewashed to eliminate any gloomy atmosphere. If the long discussed Washington Street Light Rail is ever built, it will utilize this now unused section of the subway to reach Park Street.

This view of a glistening new Boylston Street Station was taken several days before the subway opened to the public. Note that all the steel work and fencing is painted white to compliment the shining white tile walls. The track leading downgrade on the right carried cars for Roxbury, South Boston, and Dorchester underneath the Boylston Street Branch of the subway used by cars from Jamaica Plain, Brookline, and Cambridge. This now unused track could see service again for the proposed Light Rail Line along Washington Street to Dudley Street.

Here is the shiny white Park Street Station as it was photographed on August 31, 1897, before it opened for public service. On August 16, 1964, the Federal Government declared the Tremont Street Subway to be a National Historic Landmark.

A month after the subway opened, this group about to board a Jamaica Plain-Huntington Avenue car paused to allow the Transit Commission photographer to record the scene.

GROVE HALL COLUMBUS ⚡ BLUE HILL AV.		4	PEARL STREET ⚡ CAMBRIDGE.		SOMERVILLE UNION SQ ⚡ SPRING HILL.	LONGWOOD AV. ⚡ HUNTINGTON AV.
ASHMONT MILTON ⚡ CROSS TOWN.			ALLSTON PEARL ST ⚡ CAMBRIDGE.			CYPRESS ST. ⚡ BROOKLINE.
FIELDS CORNER. ⚡ CROSS TOWN.			HARVARD SQ. ⚡ CAMBRIDGE.		RESERVOIR ⚡ BEACON ST.	RESERVOIR. ⚡ BROOKLINE VILL.
MEETING HOUSE HILL ⚡	5		WATERTOWN. ⚡ MT. AUBURN.		NEWTON BLVRD. ⚡ BEACON ST.	NEWTON BLVRD. ⚡ BROOKLINE VILL.
GROVE HALL WARREN ST. ⚡ CROSS-TOWN.			WAVERLY. ⚡ MT. AUBURN.		ALLSTON VIA ⚡ COOLIDGE COR.	
FOREST HILLS. ⚡ CROSS TOWN.			MT. AUBURN. ⚡ HURON AV.	2	OAK SQ. BRIGHTON ⚡ COOLIDGE CORNER.	
JAMAICA PLAIN ⚡ CROSS-TOWN.			ARLINGTON HGTS. ⚡ HARVARD SQ.		OAK SQ. BRIGHTON ⚡ COTTAGE FARM.	
			NORTH CAMBRIDGE ⚡ HARVARD SQ.		NEWTON COTTAGE FARM ⚡ OAK SQUARE.	
			HARVARD SQ. ⚡ BROADWAY.			

A view of the electric destination board at Park Street Station shows the list of twenty-seven routes that operated from this station in 1897. In addition, another dozen routes started from Scollay Square Station, serving such diverse points as Somerville, Cambridge, Malden, Everett, Chelsea, Revere, and Lynn.

A brand-new trolley car in a brand-new subway is shown in this August 1897 photograph. Open Trolley No. 2544, which had recently been built by the Saint Louis Car Company, carried a group of supervisors and trolley conductors from the Fields Corner and Milton car barns on a training trip through the new subway. The Saint Louis Car Building Company was a leading builder of railroads, subway, and trolley cars of all types, but closed down in 1973, shortly after it had become a conglomerate.

Prior to the completion of the Park Street Station, the section of Boston Common adjoining Tremont Street was a huge mudhole with girders, bricks, and other construction material scattered about. This view looking toward Park Street Church shows the conditions on November 27, 1896. Tremont Street was never entirely closed nor was streetcar service disrupted during Boston's original "Big Dig," thanks to the careful supervision of the Transit Commission's small group of engineers, who kept tight control on the projects.

While many staid Bostonians were very critical of what they termed the desecration of the sacred Common, they were equally vocal in praise of the new subway upon its completion when they viewed stations such as Park Street, seen here on August 15, 1897, two weeks prior to opening. The station looked almost clinical with its gleaming white walls and steelwork.

Scollay Square on the morning of June 2, 1896, was busy as usual and was little disturbed by subway construction, as preliminary work had only just begun. The statue of Governor John Winthrop would soon be moved to allow evacuation work to begin. Note the streetcars bound for Columbus Avenue, Washington Avenue, Chelsea, Allston, and South Boston, as well as the wide range of commercial activity.

July 9, 1897, found the Winthrop statue moved out of the square and subway construction well under way. Among the wide assortment of wholesale dry goods and furniture firms located in or near the square were a number of cigar factories. Cigar making was at one time a big business in Boston.

On August 13, 1897, a good part of the Square was taken up with construction equipment, although traffic still flowed reasonably well. Two longtime Boston landmarks are visible in the center of this view. The famous Steaming Tea Kettle hanging over the door of the Oriental Tea Company is shown, and just to its right stands the Crawford House, opened in 1848 as a high-class hotel, but which later became famous to Navy men around the world for its entertainment, especially in the mid-twentieth century. It fell victim to the wrecking ball in 1963, when Scollay Square was remade into Government Center.

This 1906 view of Scollay Square was taken shortly after 10 am on what must have been a Sunday morning, considering the deserted aspect of the square. A lone trolley is bound for Newton via Harvard Square, while several people stand in front of the handsome granite headhouse which serves as the main entrance to the Scollay Square Subway Station.

This September 1908 view of Scollay Square looking toward Tremont Street shows the Suffolk Savings Bank building. The well-dressed ladies are standing in front of the granite entrance, which was designed by Charles Brigham, to the Scollay Square Subway Station.

The Scollay Square Station had a separate platform for cars bound for Everett, Somerville, Malden, Chelsea, and Lynn. This platform was called "Brattle," since it had its own entrance stairway at the corner of Brattle Street. In this May 1901 scene, a hack awaits passengers in front of the entrance. The sign above the hack reads: "Subway to Charlestown and Chelsea," and the Crawford House can be seen on the left.

In this view of the now vanished Adams Square, looking north towards Haymarket Square on April 13, 1897, can be seen the usual parade of streetcars. Subway construction is under way through the seeming chaos with little, if any, hindrance.

Adams Square, showing the completed subway entrance, is seen here in this December 26, 1901 photograph. Adams Square was for many years the center for the wholesale furniture and stove trade, as well as the restaurant equipment business. The square was named for Samuel Adams, a member of the Sons of Liberty and a governor of Massachusetts.

Like the similar station building in Scollay Square, the handsome Adams Square Station entrance, shown here as it appeared on May 17, 1910, was designed by Charles Brigham. The entrance was moved in 1932 because it was considered a hindrance to automobile traffic. The summer of 1963 would see every building in Adams and Scollay Squares demolished to make way for the new Government Center. Boston's "New" City Hall now stands on this site.

In 1898, Adams Square Subway Station, with a car ready to depart for Charlestown and West Somerville, was captured in this photograph. This site is now the basement garage of City Hall, where one may enter a doorway leading to an unused section of the original subway leading to Scollay Square, now occupied with utility cables.

Looking up Cornhill toward Scollay Square on April 14, 1897, this photograph shows a trolley bound for Chelsea and Malden. Notice the concentration of kitchenware and furniture dealers on the street, along with a book dealer on the left, the business for which Cornhill was renowned.

A February 8, 1897 view of Haymarket Square shows the recently closed station of the Boston and Maine Railroad, which had been replaced by an enlarged North Union Station on nearby Causeway Street. Opened on October 20, 1845, the venerable old station had been taken over by the Transit Commission and would soon be demolished to make way for the northern entrance ramp of the Tremont Street Subway.

Here, the interior of the Boston and Maine Railroad Haymarket Square Station is seen on June 23, 1897, just prior to its demolition. The transit commission, which had paid the Boston and Maine $750,000 for the station property, was using it to store construction materials when this view was taken.

This August 5, 1897 photograph shows a view looking south across Haymarket Square from the top of the old Haymarket Square Railroad Station. In little more than a year, most of the trolley cars in this view would be running beneath Haymarket Square in the new subway.

The new Haymarket Station beneath the square is shown here several days after this portion of the subway opened to public travel, with a northbound car about to leave the station. This station today is unused and cars pass through it without stopping, since a smaller station was opened by the MBTA immediately to the south of the original station.

Unlike the substantial and attractive granite entrances at the other stations of the Tremont Street Subway, the entrance at Haymarket Square was designed with an emphasis on economy, since it was felt that the installation of elevated trains in the subway in 1901 might require changes to the stairways and entrances to the station. Though this structure was designed to be of a temporary nature, it remained in use for over thirty-five years and is seen in this view taken February 19, 1934, shortly before the entrance was replaced by a more modern one.

By September 1898, the subway had been completed and was in operation. This view looking toward Haymarket Square shows cars coming and going from the north entrance to the subway. It is typical of nineteenth-century Boston that all but one of the buildings are constructed of red brick. The sole exception was the large mansard roof structure at right center known as the E.E. Gray Building, which was built of stone. It was demolished in 1963 to make room for the new Government Center.

The north entrance to the subway near Haymarket Square is seen in this May 20, 1909 photograph. The elevated trains had just been shifted from the Tremont Street Subway to the new Washington Street Tunnel, and the final track rearrangement for that change is being carried out in this view. The large brick structure atop the subway entrance is the Haymarket Relief Hospital, a downtown emergency center operated by the Boston City Hospital.

In this 1961 view of the north entrance to the subway are a pair of modern PCC-type trolleys which served the Green Line Subways for four decades. On the left, the Fitzgerald Elevated Expressway has replaced all the buildings in the earlier view. The Haymarket Relief Hospital would soon fall to the wrecking ball. As this book is going to press, work is under way on removal of the overhead expressway, which will leave the Tremont Street Subway as the only surviving structure from these photographs.

At the north end of the subway, near North Station, was a switching tower which directed the streetcars onto the proper tracks. In this March 1900 view, we see the tower with the old North Station in the background. To the left, notice the shed and pile of rails to be used for construction of the elevated line which would require removal of the switch tower. All the buildings on the right along Haverhill Street were demolished in 1955 to make way for the Fitzgerald Expressway.

The original plan of the Tremont Street Subway called for an underground loop and station at North Station. However, with the impending construction of the new elevated system, it was decided to erect a temporary surface station seen in this photo from September 14, 1899. The building with the large clock is the old North Union Station of the Boston and Maine Railroad. The stone castle-like structure on the right is the old depot of the Fitchburg Railroad. The depot featured a large public hall on the second floor. The famous Swedish singer Jenny Lind performed in the hall on October 11 and 12, 1850.

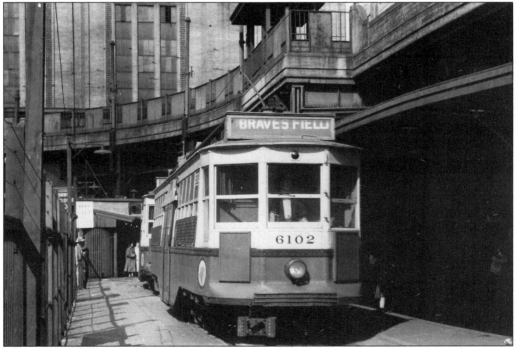

Here is a picture of the same location in 1949 with the new (1928) North Station and Boston Garden in the background and the elevated line to Lechmere Square in Cambridge curving to the left. The train of large center-entrance cars is headed for Braves Field on Commonwealth Avenue, which later became Boston University Field. These steel center-door trolleys were the most efficient type of equipment ever used on the Green Line, serving for thirty-six years.

In this interesting scene on Causeway Street at North Station on August 12, 1884, the handsome Fitchburg Depot dominates the view. The Metropolitan Sewer System, under construction at the time, required the wooden trestlework on the left side of the street for a material conveyor system. The omnibus on the left is headed for Charlestown, while the Boston and Maine Railroad locomotives crossing Causeway Street are entering and leaving the Haymarket Square Depot.

Here is a view of Causeway Street, looking from Keany Square toward North Station in August 1931. The Charlestown Elevated Line casts its shadow over the street, and the trolley car in the center, on its way from Scollay Square Station to Central Square in Lynn, has just emerged from the subway at North Station.

Over the years, several changes were made to the Tremont Street Subway section of the Green Line, including rebuilding of some stations and enlargement of others, as well as rerouting of a section of subway through Government Center. Here in August 1914 is a peaceful scene on the Mall above Park Street Station, just before construction began to enlarge the station. Notice the U.S. Weather Bureau kiosk, a fixture on the common until the 1940s.

October 1914 found the Mall above Park Street Station torn up to permit the extension of the station southward in order to handle rapidly increasing traffic through the station. St. Paul's Cathedral and the R.H. Stearns' Department Store may be seen on the right. Stearns' was later remodeled as an apartment house.

By November 17, 1914, the project to enlarge Park Street Station to better than twice its original size was well under way. During 1914, the Boston Transit System carried 343,181,049 riders. Many of these riders were funneled through Park Street Station where, beginning in 1912, the new tunnel line from Harvard Square in Cambridge terminated in a lower level beneath the original station.

To accommodate the enlargement of Park Street Station, several of the granite entrance buildings had to be placed on rollers and winched along to new locations. Designed by Wheelwright and Haven, these handsome structures were often referred to as "the public library's puppies," since they bore a resemblance to that notable structure in Copley Square.

There was no interruption to trolley car service through Park Street Station while the enlargement project was carried on. Here, on October 21, 1914, a trolley leaves Park Street Station for Dudley Street via Washington Street. This route was discontinued in March 1938. In the early 1990s, plans were made to restore the route as a replacement for the old Orange Line Elevated that ran on Washington Street.

In this late 1915 view we see the new section of Park Street Station which had been added to the southerly end of the original station. Suspended from the ceiling is a new electric indicator board listing the twenty trolley lines that ran through Park Street in 1915, when over 300,000 riders a day were carried on the Green Line.

Among the busiest years for the Green Line were the World War II years. From 1941 to 1946, 350,000 riders a day squeezed aboard cars on the eight routes using the Green Line tunnels. Here we see a crowd exiting one of the large center-entrance trolleys which were the mainstay of the Green Line service.

In this March 1959 scene, a train for Beacon Street in Brookline is loading on the left, while the crowd in the foreground is about to board an approaching train for Watertown. In June 1969, service was temporarily suspended on the Watertown Line to reduce subway congestion and was never restored.

Here, homeward-bound commuters board an Arborway-Huntington Avenue train on the evening of February 6, 1959. At Park Street, the train consisted of the modern PCC-type trolleys used on the Green Lines from 1940 to 1985. Like the Watertown Line, the Arborway Line was "temporarily" closed on December 27, 1985, and never reopened. It was the last of the Green Line routes using these PCC-type trolleys, many of which were built at the Pullman Company plant in Worcester.

Park Street Station is shown here in June of 1982 with one of the seven modern-type rail cars built by Kinki-Sharyo of Japan. These well-built cars have been highly successful and have provided the bulk of Green Line service in recent years.

A typical crowd in Scollay Square Station in the spring of 1959 is pictured here, while a train for Commonwealth Avenue loads as many riders as possible, although another train would be along in a few minutes. Behind the fence to the right was the unused Brattle Street platform, where cars formerly left for Charlestown, Everett, Somerville, Chelsea, Revere, and Lynn.

Scollay Square Station changed very little over the years, except for the addition of modern lighting and turnstiles as seen in this view of passengers boarding a Beacon Street train on March 10, 1959. Today, this station is known as Government Center. It underwent a total modernization during the summer of 1963.

During the summer of 1963, the section of subway between Scollay and Haymarket Squares northbound was realigned, eliminating the sharp curve into Adams Square. The Adams Square Station was demolished, and the Scollay Square Station was rebuilt and renamed Government Center. This view was taken July 5, 1963, and shows the new section of subway leading from the old Scollay Square Station in the center, with the Suffolk Bank above it.

Looking across what was Scollay Square toward Tremont Street, one can see the junction of the old and new sections of the subway as a train bound for Lechmere Square, Cambridge, passes through the seeming chaos of construction. The Sears Crescent is visible at the top of this photograph.

Here is a general view of what were once Scollay and Adams Squares on July 19, 1963. A remaining section of Hanover Street can be seen at the left. The new section of the subway is in the center, with Faneuil Hall at the upper right. Cornhill curves to the right, with the original northbound subway beneath it.

In this view looking northward from Scollay Square on June 4, 1963, a section of the Fitzgerald Expressway may be seen beyond the buildings in the process of being demolished. When the new section of subway in the foreground is completed, it will be covered, and this area will become part of the present City Hall Plaza. As can be seen, Boston lost a lot of interesting architecture at this time.

43

On June 11, 1963, much of Boston's red brick heritage was being lost as progress marched on with the new Government Center. The framing for the new subway is on the left, with the famous Union Oyster House, which has fortunately survived, on the right.

The southbound track was deserted on August 2, 1901, when this view was taken at Park Street, showing the high level wooden platforms and third rail power supply that were installed to permit operation of the elevated trains. Note the signs advising passengers to "Please Move Quickly," a longtime feature of Boston subway stations.

From June 1901 to November 1908, the elevated trains connecting Roxbury, downtown Boston, and Charlestown (today's Orange Line) were routed through the Tremont Street Subway until the new subway under Washington Street could be completed. Here is the entrance to the Tremont Street Subway at Shawmut Avenue and Pleasant Street on June 5, 1901, with trolley cars still operating, while preparations are under way for operation of the elevated trains to begin on June 10, 1901.

Here is the Shawmut Avenue entrance to the subway on July 2, 1901. This location was called Pleasant Street Station. An elevated train is picking up passengers for Dudley Street, in Roxbury. This section of the subway was used exclusively by the elevated trains, while other sections were shared with the trolley cars. Pleasant Street itself would vanish in a few years, becoming part of Broadway, which was extended from Washington Street to Tremont Street.

In this scene at Scollay Square we see an elevated train bound for Sullivan Square, Charlestown. A passenger could board an elevated train for Charlestown, Atlantic Avenue, and Roxbury or board trolley cars for Somerville, Everett, Malden, Chelsea, Revere, and Lynn from this busy station.

In this January 8, 1903 view at Haymarket Square Station, an attendant is demonstrating the operation of the moveable sections of the high platforms. The sections slid out to meet the doorways of the elevated cars, a necessity since the station was on a curve and a large gap existed between the platform and the side of the elevated cars.

In this view looking northward from Haymarket Square to North Station on April 30, 1901, workmen engaged in connecting the tracks from the new Charlestown Elevated Line to the Tremont Street Subway pause to look at the cameraman. Haverhill Street is to the right and Canal Street to the left. The old Boston and Maine Railroad Haymarket Square Station formerly stood on the site of the tracks in the foreground.

July 19, 1901, finds one of the new elevated trains bound for Scollay Square and Park Street Station passing trolley cars from Cambridge, Chelsea, and Chinatown at the Haymarket Square entrance to the subway. The North Station is in the distance.

Shown in this December 2, 1908 photograph are two additional tracks that had been added to carry the elevated trains into the just opened Washington Street Tunnel. In the foreground, a major rearrangement of the trolley tracks is taking place in preparation for construction of a new elevated line from North Station to Lechmere Square in East Cambridge.

On June 20, 1907, work began on an elevated line from North Station to Lechmere Square in East Cambridge. This elevated line, completed in June 1912, carried trolley cars from Cambridge and Somerville directly into the Tremont Street Subway, allowing those cars to avoid traffic-filled streets between the Charles River and North Station. In this view, the new El structure is seen curving above Causeway Street in front of the old North Union Station.

Work is well along on the Lechmere Elevated in this June 1911 photo. The building on the left with the awnings is the Haymarket Hotel, and the large mansard-roofed structure in the center is the Boston and Lowell Railroad Station, built in 1873. The large building on the right is the main entrance to the old North Station, built in 1893. A new station replaced these interesting structures in 1928.

The Lechmere Elevated Line, or Viaduct, as it became known, crossed the Charles River on a handsome concrete viaduct and drawbridge, which we see under construction in this January 1909 view. In the foreground, the empty coal barge *Boston*, from Perth Amboy, New Jersey, is being towed down the Charles River toward the harbor. Many businesses in Cambridge received bulk deliveries of coal, lumber, and stone by barge and schooner until the late 1930s.

The Lechmere Viaduct is shown here while under construction in October 1910. This view is looking toward Boston from Cambridge, and the present-day Museum of Science is located on the right side of the street, just out of the picture.

"Salt and pepper, mustard and vinegar." That time-honored playground litany is not disturbed as a train from Cambridge speeds across the Lechmere Viaduct bound for Park Street Station and beyond to Brighton and Brookline. The playground in this late 1940s view has since been replaced by a traffic rotary and the Charles River Park apartment development.

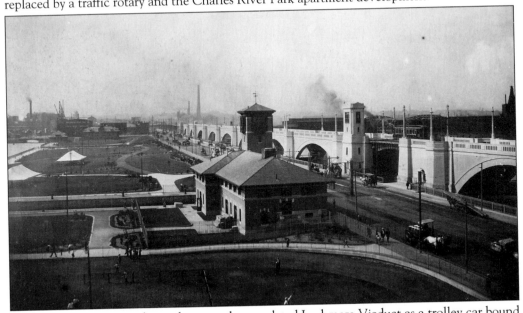

This August 1912 view shows the recently completed Lechmere Viaduct as a trolley car bound for Somerville crosses the draw-span of the viaduct. The building in the foreground housed the controls for the drawbridge for street traffic and also for the locks, allowing shipping to enter and leave the Charles River. The draw-span on the viaduct was controlled from the concrete tower just to the left of the trolley car.

An example of the Boston Elevated management's commitment to safety is seen in this May 1912 view. A brand new Type Four streetcar with a group of employees on a training trip over the new Lechmere Viaduct has stopped at a bumper device near the drawbridge on the viaduct. When the draw-span opened to allow the passage of a ship, this bumper rose automatically from the trackbed to prevent cars from approaching the open span.

In this view looking across the Charles River toward Cambridge on August 25, 1955, the nearly new Museum of Science (opposite the Lechmere Viaduct), the Leverett Circle Underpass, and the Science Park Station are visible. The new station was built to serve the Science Museum and the Charles River Park apartment complex nearby, which was in the process of replacing Boston's old West End.

This photograph looking north across the Lechmere Viaduct was taken in August 1955. The Science Park Station and Leverett Circle Underpass were both completed. The brick tenement house on the right would soon be torn down. On the horizon can be seen the large gas tanks of Eastern Gas and Fuel Company in Everett, now gone, as well as the Bunker Hill Monument and the Mystic River Bridge.

In this mid-1950s scene, a trolley train from Lechmere Square heads into the Tremont Street Subway and Brookline. On the right is an elevated train bound for the Washington Street Tunnel and Forest Hills. The old Haymarket Square Hotel is still standing next to the train on the left.

In this June 1934 photograph, a train has just emerged from the Tremont Street Subway and is rounding the curve at North Station en route to Lechmere Square. The buildings on the left along Haverhill Street were torn down in 1955 to make way for the Fitzgerald Expressway, which is itself due to be replaced by a tunnel in the late 1990s. Such is progress!

The North Station platform on the Lechmere Viaduct line is seen here in 1912, with a car (on the left) bound for Clarendon Hill in Somerville followed by an open trolley from Dudley Street in Roxbury. On the right is a car headed into the Tremont Street Subway from Somerville.

The Lechmere Elevated or Viaduct snaked through Boston's old West End above Lowell Street and is seen in this picture with a train bound from Lechmere Square to Boston College. With the exception of the Registry of Motor Vehicles building, which rises in the background, these buildings were all demolished to make way for the Charles River Park apartment complex .

In 1922 a transfer station was erected in Lechmere Square, and henceforth, all trolley cars from Somerville and Cambridge would end their route here, with passengers transferring to trains for Park Street and Kenmore Square. In this 1922 view, we see a train about to depart for Park Street and the subway.

Here is Lechmere Square in July 1911. Prior to opening the transfer station in 1922, cars from downtown Boston descended via this ramp to the street and continued on to Somerville on the right or along Cambridge Street in the center of the picture to Harvard Square. On the right, a horse-drawn watering wagon is being filled at a curbside standpipe. Once a common sight, these wagons would wet down the streets on hot summer days to reduce the amount of dust and grit blowing about.

On a bright October morning in 1946, passengers boarded a train of brand new PCC-type cars for Park Street and Beacon Street in Brookline. Most of these people arrived here at Lechmere from Cambridge and Somerville aboard electric trolley buses, a type of vehicle which once served most of Cambridge and Somerville, as well as other areas around Boston.

A cold winter day in 1941 saw riders leaving an electric trolley bus at Lechmere Station and hurrying to board a train for the Tremont Street Subway. These swift, quiet electric vehicles which replaced the trolley cars on the route from Harvard to Lechmere Squares were themselves replaced by diesel buses in 1963.

This trolley has just left the Lechmere Station and is turning from Third Street onto Cambridge Street en route to the car barns near Harvard Square in December 1935. At this time, the trolleys serving the Commonwealth Avenue Subway-Lechmere Line were stored and serviced at the car barns near Harvard Square and had to travel over Cambridge Street to reach them.

Here is a train from Harvard Square rolling along Cambridge Street to Lechmere Station to begin its run into the Tremont Street Subway and on to Brighton and Brookline. This section of East Cambridge has changed little over the years, and many of the buildings in this scene are still standing.

Two routes from the Tremont Street Subway to Harvard Square are seen in this photograph from 1915. One route ran via Lechmere Square and Cambridge Street, while the other ran via Boylston Street, Massachusetts Avenue, and Central Square. The ornate building on the right was the entrance to the Cambridge Subway, which ran directly to Park Street Station and drew many riders away from the longer trolley lines which connected Harvard Square with Park Street.

In this view of Central Square, we see an open trolley en route from Park Street Subway Station to Arlington Heights. This long route left the subway at the Public Garden and traveled over Boylston Street to Massachusetts Avenue and through Central and Harvard Squares to Arlington Heights. The opening of the Cambridge Subway (today's Red Line) in 1912 led to the discontinuance of this long route, along with others.

This interesting wooden car barn, which housed many of the trolleys operating to Harvard Square from the Tremont Street Subway, was built in August 1889 to service the first electric trolley line connecting Cambridge to Boston. It was replaced by a much larger and more modern facility in 1911.

Two

On the Rail

In March 1912, construction began on the Boylston Street Subway, which extended from a connection with the Tremont Street Subway at the Public Garden under Boylston Street and the Muddy River to a point near Kenmore Square. This subway was designed to remove the very heavily patronized trolley lines serving Beacon Street, Commonwealth Avenue, and Watertown from traffic-clogged Boylston Street, and it provided a fast ride into Park Street Station for the residents served by those lines.

The new entrance in the center of Boylston Street was completed in July 1915, and cars from Chestnut Hill, Longwood Avenue, Beacon Street, and Arborway are seen here using it. This view looking toward the Common was taken at the corner of Arlington and Boylston Streets. Automobiles outnumbered horse-drawn vehicles by a large margin by this time.

During construction of the Boylston Street Subway, temporary tracks were laid on Saint James Avenue to divert the heavy trolley car traffic from Boylston Street, between Copley and Park Squares. This 1913 photograph shows the heavy trolley traffic. Trinity Church is on the left and the Copley Plaza is on the right. The Hotel Westminster in the center later became the site for the glass-sheathed John Hancock Tower.

In this 1913 view of Saint James Avenue, we see an outbound trolley from Park Street Station headed for Dudley Street and Ashmont, while an inbound trolley of the Middlesex and Boston Street Railway Company from Newton Highlands is coming into Park Street Station. The vacant lot on the right was the site of the Boston and Providence Railroad's Park Square Depot. The Hotel Statler was built on that plot, which later became the Park Plaza.

A busy moment at the corner of Arlington and Boylston Streets was photographed in September 1913 with an interesting mix of traffic, including open summer trolleys, automobiles, and horse-drawn carriages. This view was taken looking from the steps of the Arlington Street Church.

In this view of Boylston Street, looking east from the lawn of the Natural History Museum, the trolley cars have not yet been diverted to Saint James Avenue, although piles of construction material for the new subway line the curb. Some of the buildings in this view still exist. The Natural History Museum would later evolve into the Museum of Science, now located on the Charles River Dam.

In June 1913, Boylston Street was rather messy due to the ongoing subway construction. In this photo the streetcars have been diverted onto Saint James Avenue and are passing on the other side of Trinity Church, which is seen on the right. Hugh Nawn, owner of the construction equipment in the foreground, was a major contractor at this time and was responsible for building most of the Cambridge and Boylston Street Subways.

This view of Boylston Street looking toward Copley Square on a warm July day in 1913 finds an open trolley en route to Fenway Park with a crowd of baseball fans riding on the side running board. The Hotel Lenox is on the right, and the Public Library is visible in the distance.

In this June 1912 photograph, we see an open trolley car on Route 940 to Beacon Street in Brookline, which is now the 'C' Route of the Green Line. Visible in the distance is the Hotel Lenox. To the right, above the passenger coach storage yards of the Boston and Albany Railroad, is the Copley Square Hotel. The Prudential Center now occupies the site of the former railroad yards.

This August 6, 1912 photograph shows an outbound trolley on Boylston Street. On the corner is the Henley-Kimball Company, which sold Hudson Motor Cars, and next door is an agency for Stutz cars. The auto sales agencies which lined Boylston Street during this period were eventually concentrated at Kenmore Square. By World War II, all these dealers had moved beyond Kenmore Square along both sides of Commonwealth Avenue, which became known as Automobile Row.

Looking on Boylston Street from the Hotel Lenox on October 3, 1912, one can see the Boston and Albany Railroad Yards on the left. The majority of the buildings on the right are still standing, and the trolley car in the foreground, No. 396 of the Boston Elevated Railway, is also still in existence; it is preserved in a transit museum.

This October 1912 photograph shows the Boston and Albany Railroad Yards on the right side of Boylston Street. Commuter and Amtrak trains still run past this area but are now underground. The coach yards of the railroad are now the site of the Prudential Center and the War Memorial (Hynes) Auditorium. Many of the buildings on the left side of Boylston Street are still standing and provide an interesting contrast to the modern construction across the street.

As the Boylston Street Subway approached Massachusetts Avenue, it veered toward Commonwealth Avenue, passing under Newbury Street, Massachusetts Avenue, the Back Bay Fens, and private property, in order to enter Kenmore Square under Commonwealth Avenue. Here we see the shell of the subway from atop a building on Newbury Street, where a station called Massachusetts was built, with a surface level station directly above the subway station.

The surface level of Massachusetts Station had two entrances for trolley cars—one on Boylston Street and one on Newbury Street—with the cars running through the building. This April 1920 photograph was taken looking through the station toward Newbury Street as passengers board cars for Chestnut Hill, Dudley Street, and Harvard Square. The stairway in the center gave access to the lower level subway station.

In this June 6, 1939 scene, a car bound for Arborway is leaving the Boylston Street end of Massachusetts Station. The Arborway cars had been diverted to the upper level of this station due to a parade which had closed off sections of Huntington Avenue and Boylston Street on the day this picture was taken. This building was demolished to permit construction of the Massachusetts Turnpike Extension into Boston.

This July 1912 photograph was taken looking from the Eastgate of the Back Bay Fens toward Commonwealth Avenue. The subway passed under the Muddy River near this point, and extensive waterproofing measures were required as a result.

Inasmuch as the Boylston Street Subway was situated in the marsh-filled land of the Back Bay, in addition to passing under the Muddy River near Kenmore Square, waterproofing was a matter of great importance. Here we see workmen applying sheets of felt saturated with tar to the roof of the subway prior to back-filling with earth and gravel up to street level.

As originally built, the Boylston Street Subway came to the surface at the junction of Beacon Street and Commonwealth Avenue at the in-town edge of Kenmore Square—or Governor's Square as it was known in 1912, when this view was taken from the roof of a building on Beacon Street looking in-town. The still-unfinished subway entrance can be seen in the center of the Commonwealth Avenue Mall.

October 2, 1914, was a bright fall day, and Major-General William Bancroft, president of the Boston Elevated Railway, provided two new Type-Four trolley cars to carry his invited friends and public officials on an inspection trip through the new Boylston Street Subway, which would open to the public on the following day. In this view at the subway entrance, General Bancroft (fifth from the left) is reaching into his left coat pocket, probably for a subway token!

Here is the original Boylston Street Subway entrance on Commonwealth Avenue, just east of Kenmore Square, on October 2, 1914. When the subway was extended westward under Kenmore Square in 1931–1932, this entrance was closed, but a section including the arched top was retained for ventilation purposes and still may be seen today behind a screen of shrubs.

The necessity for extending the Boylston Street Subway through Kenmore Square to new exit ramps on Commonwealth Avenue and Beacon Street to the west of the square was brought about by increasingly heavy traffic. This early 1931 photograph shows the streetcars heading for the Boylston Street Subway as they contend with heavy automobile traffic.

This early 1931 view of Kenmore Square shows construction under way on the new Kenmore Square Subway Station, although with no interruption to streetcar service. The parade of trolleys are on the routes to Lake Street in Newton, to Watertown, and to Beacon Street in Brookline. Upon completion of the subway station, the name "Kenmore Square" was adopted in place of Governor Square.

Kenmore Square was an attractive green island that replaced the entrance to the Boylston Street Subway. The buses picked up passengers at the sidewalks where the stairways to the subway are located. Traffic is somewhat light because gasoline was being rationed when this view was taken in 1943.

In November of 1943, the lawn over the subway and in the center of Kenmore Square gave way to a bus station in order to handle increased bus traffic to the Kenmore Subway Station. This view looking eastward was taken just prior to the start of construction on a larger bus station.

This photograph of Kenmore Square in April 1968 finds the new bus station nearly completed. A larger bus station had to be built due to the conversion of the Watertown-Park Street Trolley Line to buses, which required large numbers of passengers to transfer to the subway at Kenmore.

After passing through the new Kenmore Square Subway Extension, trains for Lake Street (now Boston College) and Watertown emerged from the subway on Commonwealth Avenue at Blandford Street. Trains for Beacon Street in Brookline came to the surface on Beacon Street at Saint Mary's Street. Here we see a Fenway Park-bound train leaving the Commonwealth Avenue Subway entrance.

In this view looking on Commonwealth Avenue during an afternoon rush hour in 1937, we see a line of trolleys carrying homeward-bound commuters to Lake Street and Watertown. This scene is near the Cottage Farm Bridge, now known as the Boston University Bridge.

Until the Boston Braves baseball team moved to Milwaukee, a major source of traffic for Commonwealth Avenue trolleys was Braves Field, seen here with crowds arriving at the park. Located just off Commonwealth Avenue, Braves Field was purchased by Boston University and, after a face-lift, continues in use as a stadium for college sports.

This September 1948 view shows a rather quiet moment along Commonwealth Avenue as an outbound train rolls along to Watertown. Formerly a center for automobile dealerships, this section of Commonwealth Avenue is now occupied by a number of Boston University facilities.

In this photograph from 1900, this trolley from Oak Square in Brighton is heading for the Tremont Street Subway. Except for the two stately homes on the right, a rural atmosphere pervades the avenue because extensive development was still many years in the future.

On January 10, 1905, this two-car train from Oak Square in Brighton moved along Boylston Street near Copley Square en route to the Park Street Subway Station. The lead car, No. 529, was built by the Newburyport Car Company of Newburyport, Massachusetts, which was at one time a supplier of trolley cars to many New England transit systems.

Apparently, someone brought their new Brownie Kodak camera into work at the Watertown Car House on summer day in 1914 and persuaded the trolley operators to ham it up for the camera. The three gentlemen on the front platform of Open Car 3223 are the epitome of dignity.

A beaming father has "junior" posing in front of a large new trolley and wearing someone's uniform hat and jacket, which are obviously a bit too large!

The former Boston Elevated Railway Company was well equipped to deal with winter storms. Here an electric snow sweeper prepares to leave the Watertown yards to clear the tracks as far as the subway entrance at Kenmore Square. Equipped with powerful rotating brushes which threw the snow clear of the tracks, these cars were a common sight on Boston streets during winter storms.

In 1940, the Boston Elevated Railway Company began to purchase the new-style PCC trolleys for use on the Green Line Subway System. The first route to receive them was the Watertown-Park Street Subway Line. Here, one of the new trolleys pauses at Newton Corner en route to Park Street on May 18, 1941. The name "PCC" was derived from the President's Conference Committee of Transit Companies, which got together to oversee the design of a modern trolley for use in the United States and Canada.

The Watertown trolley line passed through pleasant residential areas of Newton and Brighton en route to Park Street Station in downtown Boston. Here we see an inbound car at Park and Elmwood Streets in Newton.

Here we see a Park Street Subway-bound trolley on Galen Street in Watertown near Watertown Square passing the Watertown Movie House in November of 1934. The 7:45 pm show featured John Barrymore in *Twentieth Century* and admission was only a quarter!

Good track maintenance is a necessity for safe, efficient trolley operation. Here we see new track being installed on the Watertown Line on Brighton Avenue, just west of Packard's Corner, where the Watertown and Boston College Lines branched from one another. Packard's Corner took its name from a large Packard automobile dealership once located at that intersection.

In this August 1906 photo, a trolley is crossing a temporary wooden bridge at Watertown Square, while a new bridge over the Charles River is being built. Note the ad on the front of the car for Norumbega Park, once one of New England's most popular amusement parks. Trolleys ran directly from Park Street Subway Station to the park. Those cars displayed a blue flag with a large letter "N" so people could easily identify them.

The Commonwealth Avenue Line, or Route "B" of today's Green Line, traverses some of the steepest hills on the entire transit system. This 1936 photograph shows cars descending the steep grade at Commonwealth Avenue and Carol Street. All the vacant land in the photograph has since been developed.

A track crew using an electric trolley crane car to replace worn rails attracts young observers on Commonwealth Avenue in 1938. One could bring his/her car to the Aberdeen Garage on the right and get it lubricated for seventy-five cents or take the trolley downtown for a dime.

In this August 10, 1927 view, we see a Commonwealth Avenue train inbound to Park Street Station with every seat occupied as more riders board. Most of the upscale apartment houses are equipped with their summer awnings to deflect the sun and showers from open windows, a common practice prior to air conditioning.

On a chilly February day in 1931, at the corner of Commonwealth and Harvard Avenues, a two-car train from Allston is headed for the busy Dudley Street Elevated Terminal. The heavily patronized Allston-Dudley Trolley crossed five lines that operated into the Green Line subways—Watertown, Commonwealth Avenue, Beacon Street, Huntington Avenue, and Tremont Street—and provided free transfer to those routes, a long-forgotten convenience for Boston Transit riders.

In August of 1945, the Boston Elevated Company began operating its new PCC cars in two- and three-car trains on the Beacon Street and Commonwealth Avenue routes. Here is a two-car train which has just emerged from the subway on Commonwealth Avenue at Blandford Street. The white-shirted gentleman on the left, a supervisor with the railway company, was assigned to correct any problems with the new cars.

The Commonwealth Avenue Line from Park Street terminates at Commonwealth Avenue and Lake Street on the Newton-Boston line. The original terminal was in the middle of Commonwealth Avenue, as seen in this January 1906 view. Connection was made here with the Middlesex and Boston Street Railway, serving Newton and Waltham. One of that company's cars is seen here en route to Park Street Station from Newton Highlands.

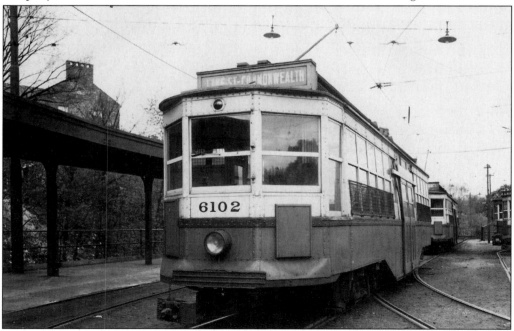

In 1930 the Middlesex and Boston System substituted its trolleys with buses, and the Boston Elevated completed a new station and car-storage yard on the north side of Commonwealth Avenue, replacing the station that had been located in the middle of the street. Formerly called Lake Street Station, it was renamed Boston College Station in 1947.

This September 1901 view looks inbound on Beacon Street toward Kenmore Square at the bridge over the Boston and Albany Railroad tracks. Trolley No. 3221 is inbound from Reservoir, or Cleveland Circle, on what is today's Green Line Route "C"-Beacon Street. The trolleys today run in a subway under the section of Beacon Street into Kenmore Station from Saint Mary's Station.

On October 23, 1932, the Kenmore Square Subway extension opened to travel, eliminating trolley car operation through the automobile-congested square. Here on the day after the opening of the extension, a train from Beacon Street in Brookline is about to enter the new subway ramp at Saint Mary's Station for a fast ride under the busy square.

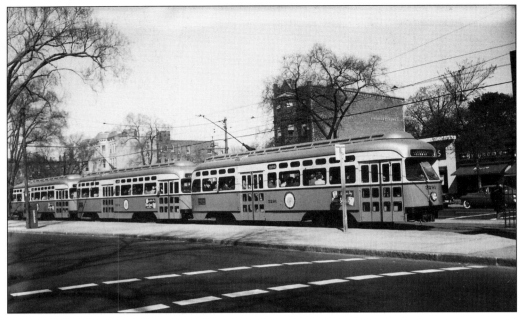

Another view at the subway entrance on Beacon Street and Saint Mary's Station from May 3, 1951, shows a train of brand new PCC cars en route to Park Street and Lechmere Square. This last group of PCC cars to be purchased was comprised of deluxe models designed especially for Boston and built by the Pullman-Standard Company at their Worcester plant.

Prior to the introduction of modern PCC cars to the Beacon Street Line in 1943, these trains of large center-entrance trolleys provided the bulk of the service. They moved crowds more quickly and efficiently than the more comfortable PCC cars did and were not retired until 1953. Here we see a train moving through Coolidge Corner in 1921, with the landmark building of the S.S. Pierce and Company grocery and importing firm dominating the scene.

Rolling inbound on Beacon Street, this train is heading for Park Street Station and then on to Lechmere Square in Cambridge. Beacon Street was the centerpiece of developer Henry M. Whitney's Brookline real estate scheme, with two roadways and a tree-lined green space in the center with provision for two trolley tracks and a trotting path for horses. The automobile on the right is parked on what was the trotting path.

Here is a rather traffic-free view of Beacon Street in 1932 with an outward bound train headed for Reservoir, known today as Cleveland Circle. Over the years, Whitney's Beacon Street has managed to retain much of its upscale residential character and integrity, a bit more so than Commonwealth Avenue which parallels it from Kenmore Square out to Chestnut Hill Avenue.

This photograph must have been taken on a Sunday morning, judging from the lack of activity at Coolidge Corner, as a single empty trolley runs deadhead to the car barns at Reservoir at the end of Beacon Street in February 1938. The handsome building towering above the trolley was built by S.S. Pierce and Company, purveyor of premium and imported foods and liquors and one of Boston's leading companies.

At Coolidge Corner in October 1930, an inbound train stopped at the ornate waiting shelters, long a landmark at Coolidge Corner and of the same style as another set of shelters which once served trolley and bus passengers in the center of Brookline Village. The trolley track crossing from left to right in this view connected Dudley Street with Allston by way of Brookline.

Here is a view of the outer end of Beacon Street at the Reservoir, now called Cleveland Circle. This view was taken in 1889, shortly after electric trolley operation began on Beacon Street, and shows a rather desolate winter scene with only one house on the left.

Even dignified Beacon Street was not immune from intrusions by the large repair trolleys and work crews who have ensured that Beacon Street riders have a safe and smooth ride into downtown Boston. Here a work crew is replacing worn rails on Beacon Street near Washington Street as an outbound train approaches.

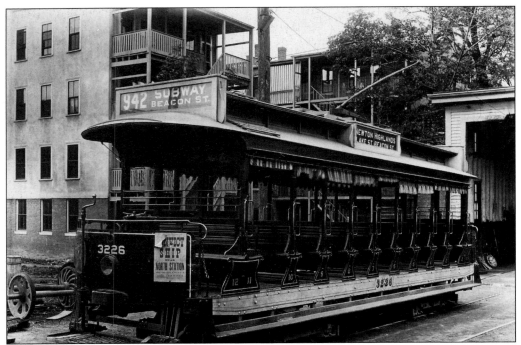

This open trolley car at the Reservoir car-house in 1912 was assigned to the long route running from Park Street Station out Beacon Street, Chestnut Hill Avenue, and over Commonwealth Avenue using the tracks of the Middlesex and Boston Street Railway Company to reach Newton Highlands. The last of these open summer cars, always popular with Boston riders, was retired in October of 1919.

Here is a view of the old car-house located at Reservoir at the end of Beacon Street in 1897. With only slight changes, this building was used to house and service the Beacon Street and Commonwealth Avenue trolleys for decades. Built in 1891, it was demolished and replaced by a modern maintenance facility in 1984.

Of the three Green Line trolley routes which funnel through Kenmore Square and the Boylston Street Subway to Park Street, the Highland Branch to Riverside has the most unique history. It was a former commuter railroad line of the Boston and Albany Railroad which was converted to light rail or trolley operation in 1959. Here we see an inbound train hauled by a steam locomotive at Newton Center in 1938.

Pictured here in 1960 is a PCC trolley outbound to Riverside as it stops at Newton Center Station, one of the few handsome stone stations to survive along the line. Built in 1891, it resembles several other stations on the line which were designed by Henry Hobson Richardson, although Newton Center itself was built to designs by Shepley, Rutan, and Coolidge.

This photograph was taken at Brookline Village in July 1955. The red-brick station on the right was built in 1878 to replace the original wooden station, which had been erected in 1847. This was the only brick station on the Highland Branch, as all the other station buildings were built of stone. Most station buildings were demolished in 1958 and were replaced by simple shelters.

Here, a PCC train inbound to Park Street picks up a passenger at Brookline Village on April 17, 1961. The conversion of the Highland Branch from railroad to light-rail operation was a notable accomplishment of the Metropolitan Transit Authority, because the 12-mile line was completed a month ahead of schedule and several thousand dollars under budget, the last time that was to happen on a Boston Transit project!

Here is the handsome stone railroad station at Reservoir, which adjoined the Reservoir trolley car yards. Built in 1887, the station was torn down in 1958 to permit regrading and the installation of new trolley tracks connecting the yard to the Highland Branch.

Here is the revamped Reservoir yard and station in 1964 with passengers waiting to board an outbound train to Riverside. The passengers are standing on the site of the old railroad station, which has been totally rearranged and is virtually unrecognizable in its modern state.

The Highland Branch was connected to the Green Line Subway under Beacon Street between Saint Mary's Street and Kenmore Square. The work is nearing completion in this early 1959 scene. As workmen stand aside, a Beacon Street train bound for Lechmere Square passes the new connecting track stacked on the left.

The 1959 conversion of the Highland Branch Line from Commuter Rail to light rail with much more frequent service proved to be a big success, with ridership increasing from 1,500 to 15,000 per day within a few months. Here is a homeward-bound crowd of commuters at Park Street Station waiting to board a Riverside train.

One of the large double-dial clocks installed at Park Street Station was made in 1897 by the E. Howard Clock Company of Boston and was used until the 1950s. The original cost of the eight clocks was $175.00 per clock. The clocks were hand-wound pendulum clocks kept in repair and wound by the Howard Clock Company. (Courtesy of David Rooney.)

For thirty-five years the Green Line was served by the PCC-type trolley, which had been designed as part of a joint effort by the leading American car builders and "big city" transit systems to provide a modern, rugged, and economical trolley car for the U.S. transit rider. This effort proved to be a great success, with PCC trolleys eventually serving many U.S. and Canadian cities for more than forty years. Here is a PCC train inbound at Reservoir Station.

As the PCC cars began to wear out, Boston, along with the San Francisco Transit System, decided to purchase new European-built trolleys. However, under pressure from the federal government, both Boston and San Francisco were forced to buy their new trolleys from the Boeing-Vertol Company, a helicopter manufacturing company. A train of Boeing light-rail cars is shown in this view of Waban Station on the Highland Branch.

The new light-rail cars provided by the Boeing-Vertol Helicopter Company turned out to be a very costly failure for both the Boston and San Francisco rail systems. Boston was forced to quickly overhaul the aging PCC cars and to purchase one hundred well-designed "Type Seven" cars from the Kinki-Sharyo Company of Japan. Here, two trains of these efficient cars are pictured at Waban Station on the "D" Highland Branch.

Only three of the attractive old stone railroad stations survived the conversion of the Highland Branch Railroad Line to a light-rail line. Here is the now unused Woodland Station, designed by H.H. Richardson and built in 1886. It now serves as a toolhouse for the Woodland Golf Course.

The Highland Branch opened for service as a light-rail line on the morning of Sunday, July 4, 1959, when the first train left Riverside for Park Street Station. Thousands of Boston and Newton residents rode the new line out of curiosity on that first day. Here, a crowd waits to board a train for Boston at Riverside.

The Highland Branch addition to the Green Line System was successful beyond all expectations, and the MTA soon had to assign additional trains to the line. The original small yard and station built at Riverside had to be enlarged to handle the additional cars, which are seen in this December 1960 view. The sand and gravel plant on the hill was soon replaced by a hotel.

After the Boylston Street Subway had been opened in 1914 to accommodate the Beacon Street, Commonwealth Avenue, and Watertown Lines, the cars from Arborway and Huntington Avenue continued to exit the subway at the old Public Garden entrance, seen here in September 1937. In order to reach Huntington Avenue, the Arborway cars traveled along Boylston Street and across Copley Square, encountering ever-increasing automobile traffic.

This April 1937 view shows a congested Boylston Street, with the Arlington Street Church on the left. To remove the streetcars from this daily traffic jam, work began on the Huntington Avenue Subway on September 18, 1937. Extending from a connection with the Boylston Street Subway at Copley Square to a point near Northeastern University, the new subway opened on February 16, 1941.

With the opening of the new Huntington Avenue Subway, the surface-car tracks were removed from Berkeley Street, Boylston Street, and Copley Square, as well as most of Huntington Avenue near downtown. Here in June 1941, the unused tracks are being removed near the old subway entrance. The Public Garden and the Arlington Street Church are on the right, while the old Greyhound Bus Terminal is on the left.

This photograph looking toward Copley Square from Berkeley Street was taken on August 4, 1941. The now unused rails are being removed from Boylston Street, while the finishing touches are being put on the New England Mutual Life Insurance Building on the right.

This January 1936 photograph shows outbound Huntington Avenue trolleys crossing Copley Square from Boylston Street onto Huntington Avenue.

In this June 1937 view looking down Huntington Avenue into Copley Square, an inbound Huntington Avenue train is about to enter the square and pass Trinity Church, on the left. All the interesting buildings seen behind the train are now gone, and the site is now occupied by one end of the Copley Place development.

Here, an open trolley car is en route to Copley Square and City Point in South Boston. The impressive structure behind the trolley is the Mechanics Building, a large exhibition hall and convention center built in 1881 for the Massachusetts Charitable Mechanic Association. The first major structure to be built on Huntington Avenue, it was torn down to make way for the Prudential Center development.

On Christmas Day in 1903, a trolley bound for Park Street Station stopped to pick up a group of people who had just emerged from the Mechanics Building, where they were given holiday food baskets by the Salvation Army. The only building in this view that is still standing today is the Copley Square Hotel, in the distance on the left.

For many years a Boston tradition was the annual parade of Boston Schoolboy Cadets, which usually took place during the first week of June, when over seven thousand neatly-uniformed boys marched from Copley Square through Boylston, Beacon, and Tremont Streets.

The Boston Elevated Company provided ninety-one trolley cars and sixty buses to the Boston School Department for the 1933 parade, which began on Huntington Avenue at the Mechanics Building. Huntington Avenue and one section of Boylston Street would be closed to traffic to allow the layover of the special trolleys and buses during the parade.

In this scene on Boylston Street, the normally traffic-clogged street is devoted to pedestrians and chartered trolley cars lined up to carry the boys home from the Schoolboy Cadet Parade in June 1939.

Looking toward Copley Square from Massachusetts Avenue, this 1926 view of Huntington Avenue shows an Arborway-bound trolley passing an inbound car in front of the once very popular Strand Theater. This section of Huntington Avenue was lined with an eclectic selection of tea rooms, used bookstores, and antique shops where one could spend an interesting Saturday afternoon.

In this early 1940 scene on Huntington Avenue, an Arborway-bound train passes the Mechanics Building, subway construction is proceeding beneath the surface of Huntington Avenue, and the surface of the avenue itself is being restored. With the exception of the Copley Square Hotel, all the buildings seen here are gone, with the Prudential Center now on the left and Copley Place on the right.

The corner of Huntington and Massachusetts Avenues, which is dominated by Symphony Hall, was a busy streetcar junction until the subway under Huntington Avenue opened. In this 1939 view a car is turning onto Massachusetts Avenue en route to City Point in South Boston.

Subway construction work is evident in this 1940 view of Huntington Avenue, with the Boston YMCA and Northeastern University buildings visible at the upper left. The long low building on the right housed Raymor Ballroom, Play-Mor Dance Hall, and other night spots and cabarets popular during this big band era.

This is Huntington Avenue in front of the YMCA Building. The trolley tracks are supported on a steel and wood trestle so as not to interrupt service during subway construction. On the right is a Hayes-Bickford Cafeteria, part of a large chain of restaurants in the Boston area which served a full line of hot meals and desserts prior to the era of fast food.

On the bright cold morning of February 16, 1941, a big crowd gathered at the unfinished entrance ramp to the new Huntington Avenue Subway to listen to speeches from officials. The officials then boarded the first train to run into the new subway, which we see in this view.

After completion of the Huntington Avenue Subway, trolleys continued to stop at the main entrance to the Mechanics Building in a modern, attractive subway station rather than on the street. Here we see a Park Street-bound train stopping at the suitably named "Mechanics Station." The new subway station serving Symphony Hall was named "Symphony."

The station name "Mechanics" became obsolete when the old Mechanics Building was replaced by the new Prudential Center, and the MBTA renamed the station "Prudential." Here, on December 3, 1964, MBTA board member George Anderson, MBTA General Manager Thomas McLernon, and two Prudential Insurance officials are shown at the name-changing ceremony.

After leaving the subway at Northeastern University, the Arborway trolleys continue out Huntington Avenue on a center reservation to Brigham Circle, where this view looking inbound was taken. On the left is the House of the Good Shepherd Home for Girls, and just beyond it is the Martin Grammar School.

In March of 1987, Brigham Circle presented a quite up-to-date scene with new Japanese-built Type-Seven rail cars, pictured here in front of some of the modern apartment houses that are occupied by members of the nearby educational and medical institutions.

At the junction of South Huntington Avenue and Heath Street is the trolley loop that was built on the site of a gas station. The operation of trolleys beyond this point was "temporarily suspended" in December 1985.

Shown in this 1897 view taken at the old car-house on South Street is an early type of electric car used on the Arborway Line. This car was built in 1891 by the West End Street Railway, which spliced together two small horsecars and installed electrical equipment—an economical way of utilizing obsolete equipment. This car was retired in 1919.

The Arborway-Huntington Avenue Line originally terminated at this wooden car-house on South Street, located next to Saint Thomas Aquinas Church in Jamaica Plain. The property continued to serve as a trolley terminal until 1949, when the property was sold and a housing project was built on the site.

The Park Street-Arborway Line's outer terminal was on Washington Street near the Forest Hills Elevated Terminal, and it was a major terminal and transfer point for all the trolley and motorbus lines serving Jamaica Plain and West Roxbury.

Cars operating from Park Street out Huntington Avenue to Cypress Street and Chestnut Hill passed through Brookline Village and stopped at the ornate station located in the center of Brookline Village's square. Nearly identical to the trolley waiting station still in use at Coolidge Corner, it was removed in 1938 to speed up automobile traffic flow through the square.

The trolleys operating on the Chestnut Hill and Cypress Street Lines from the subway were housed in this attractive car-house at Cypress and Sewell Streets in Brookline. Built in 1894, it was closed in 1933, when buses replaced the trolleys due to construction of the Worcester Turnpike, and was torn down in December 1934.

Up until 1938, three rail lines exited the Tremont Street Subway at the ramp at Tremont Street and Broadway (formerly Pleasant Street). These routes ran to Dudley Street via Washington Street, Egleston Square via Tremont Street, and City Point in South Boston via Broadway. Here is one of the large Type-Four trolleys at Tremont and Broadway en route to Dudley Street.

Here is a trolley inbound from Dudley Street under the Elevated at Massachusetts Avenue. These trolleys followed a route virtually identical to the one being planned for the new Washington Street Light Rail Line in the 1990s. Note the Puritan Movie House on the left, a longtime South End Entertainment Center.

The Subway-Washington Street-Dudley Street Line terminated here at Dudley Street Station. Shown here is the Warren Street entrance to the station, with a trolley from Park Street approaching on the right. To the right of the station entrance is Ferdinand's Furniture Company, the well-known "Blue Store," a longtime Roxbury fixture.

The route from Park Street Station out to Egleston Square exited the subway at Broadway and Tremont Street, where this view was taken on September 26, 1938. This trolley followed Tremont Street to Roxbury Crossing, then along Columbus Avenue to Egleston Square.

In this 1937 view, an Egleston Square train has just passed Union Park. Just behind the train on the left side of Tremont Street is the old Park House Hotel, once a fashionable hostelry and which is still standing. Just beyond the hotel looms the National Theatre, which was demolished in 1996.

Tremont at Northampton Street was a busy trolley junction. This March 1940 photograph shows cars heading in various directions in front of the building which once housed the Chickering Piano Works.

This is an April 1932 photograph of Tremont Street, looking toward Northampton Street. This scene has changed little over the years, except for the absence of trolley tracks and granite paving blocks. Nearly all the buildings in this view, including the old Chickering Piano Factory building on the left, are still in existence.

This interesting building at the corner of Tremont and West Lenox Streets is the Lenox Street Car House. Built during the Civil War era, this building served as the Tremont Market and later as the Boston Skating Rink. It was purchased by the Metropolitan Horse Railroad and converted into a horsecar barn in April 1877. In 1890, it was adapted for use by electric trolleys and was closed and demolished in 1934.

After the large car-house at Lenox Street was demolished in 1934, the mostly vacant property continued to be used by the maintenance department of the Boston Elevated Company. However, in June of 1956 a trolley and bus transfer yard, seen here, was opened on the site. This facility was closed in November 1961, and the property was sold for private development.

The junction of Tremont Street and Columbus Avenue was known as Roxbury Crossing, since the tracks of the Old Colony, later New Haven, crossed Tremont Street at grade. During 1895–1896, the railroad line was elevated through Roxbury to eliminate numerous grade crossings. Here we see a trolley passing the Roxbury Crossing Railroad Station, which was built in 1888. In 1895, the station was raised twenty feet to the level of the new grade, and a new lower floor was built.

A longtime South Boston landmark, the Broadway Bridge spans Fort Point Channel and the Dover Street Yards of Amtrak and the MBTA. Here, a City Point trolley is about to cross the movable swing-span, which at one time allowed shipping to navigate up Fort Point Channel as far as Southampton Street.

This photograph, taken looking east at Perkins Square in South Boston in 1915, shows trolleys bound for North Station and City Point.

This 1936 view of Perkins Square shows the junction of East and West Broadway and Dorchester Street. Perkins Square could be considered the heart of South Boston, from the commercial and traffic standpoints.

On a warm August afternoon in 1929, a trolley bound for City Point discharged passengers at Broadway and K Street. Most of East Broadway was once lined with large elm trees that provided summer shade until they fell victim to Dutch Elm Disease in the late 1940s.

This trolley has just turned off Marine Road onto East Sixth Street to start its trip to Dudley Street Station in Roxbury in August of 1938. The trolleys, brick paving, gas lights, and elm trees in this photo are all long gone, although the houses are still intact.

Here is a section of the City Point Car House in March of 1892, with a trolley about to depart for Harvard Square in Cambridge. Note the heavy fur coat worn by the trolley operator, who had to brave the elements on the open-front platform. This section of the car-house, formerly a stable, lost most of its roof in the 1938 hurricane and was torn down as a result, with trolleys then being stored outdoors.

Most of the trolleys exiting the Tremont Street Subway at North Station and bound for points north traveled through City Square in Charlestown, which is shown in this view taken in September 1899 as construction on the Charlestown Elevated was about to begin.

In this view looking toward the Navy Yard, an inbound trolley from Chelsea is seen in front of the large brick grain elevator of the Boston and Maine Railroad.

Two trolley routes traversed Charlestown between City Square and Sullivan Square. One route ran via Main Street, and the other went over Bunker Hill.

Notice the cobblestone paving Bunker Hill Street and the closely-built houses in this photograph of 1920.

This June 1938 view looking down Bunker Hill Street toward Sullivan Square shows one of the "speed traps" designed to slow down errant motorists.

Here, an open trolley is en route to Sullivan Square on Warren Street near Thompson Square in Charlestown. Most of this route was over Main Street, except for a short section between City Square and Thompson Square where the narrowness of Main Street at that point required one-way operation, as seen in this August 1914 view.

This view looking toward Warren Street from the platform of the Thompson Square Elevated Station in Charlestown was taken the morning after the Saint Valentine's Day Blizzard of February 1940. The Charlestown Elevated Line was the only public transit operating in the area the morning after that memorable storm.

When this April 1948 view of a Scollay Square-bound trolley running under the El on Main Street was taken, the trolleys had only a few months left to run until buses were put on the route. The Charlestown El Line closed in April 1975.

During the warm months of spring and summer, the popular open trolleys provided most of the car service in Boston. Here is one such car used on the long route from Broadway in Everett to City Point in South Boston via Charlestown and the Tremont Street Subway.

Charlestown residents living along or near Main Street had a choice of riding the Elevated or a trolley car to reach the North Station and downtown Boston. Here a trolley bound for Sullivan Square passes through Thompson Square in the shadow of the El Line.

One of the large Type-Three trolleys which once served the Tremont Street Subway is about to leave Clarendon Hill in Somerville for the Scollay Square Subway Station in Boston in this 1913 view. Somerville residents were served by two routes into the subway: one via Somerville Avenue and the other via Highland Avenue.

Medford residents could board a trolley at the Scollay Square Station for Salem Street in Medford. Leaving the subway at North Station, this lengthy route passed through Charlestown, over Winter Hill in Somerville, and through Medford Square to Salem Street, where this view was taken in October 1897. This site is now occupied by an MBTA bus garage.

Until January 13, 1935, the Eastern Massachusetts Street Railway operated five long trolley routes out of Scollay Square Subway Station to North Shore points such as Chelsea, Revere Beach, Lynn, and Salem. Here we see a trolley in front of Saint Rose's Church in Chelsea, en route to the Beachmont section of Revere.

The lengthy trolley routes from Salem and Lynn into the Scollay Square Subway Station traversed the business centers of Lynn, Revere, and Chelsea en route to the Tremont Street Subway. However, between Lynn and Revere, the cars crossed the Lynn Marsh, where this trolley was photographed moving at high speed toward Revere and Boston.

The Eastern Massachusetts Street Railway ran a special fast line of trolleys known as the Salem Limiteds from Salem Square into the Scollay Square Subway Station. These cars made only a few stops en route. The stops were at Central Square, Lynn, and Chelsea Square. Here, a Boston Limited is shown at Central Square in Lynn.

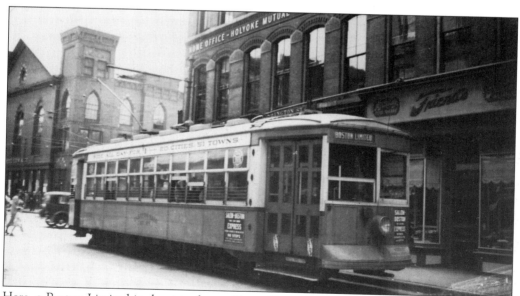

Here, a Boston Limited is about to depart Town House Square in Salem for Lynn and Scollay Square in Boston. Note the advertisement on the trolley promoting "ride all day for $1.00" tickets, a real bargain during the Depression-era thirties. On the right is a "Friends" Food Shop, once a popular chain of stores noted for their Boston baked beans.

The newsstand at Park Street Station had everything in reading material for a trip on the trolley. From local newspapers to magazines such as *Scribner's*, *The Century*, *Bohemian*, and *The Ledger Monthly*, these newsstands were an integral part of the stations. (Courtesy of David Rooney.)

Acknowledgments

We would like to thank several people for their assistance in researching this book on the centennial of Boston's Trolley System. In most instances, the photographs used in this book are from the collection of Frank J. Cheney. We greatly appreciate the help following for their support and interest in this photographic history:

Daniel J. Ahlin, the late Ray L. Ammidown (staff photographer for the Boston Elevated Railway), our editor Jamie Carter, the late Charles A. Duncan, and David Rooney.